salmonpoetry

HELLO, STEPHEN

Stephen Roger Powers

Published in 2014 by
Salmon Poetry
Cliffs of Moher, County Clare, Ireland
Website: www.salmonpoetry.com
Email: info@salmonpoetry.com

Copyright © Stephen Roger Powers, 2014

ISBN 978-1-908836-66-3

All rights reserved. No part of this publication may be reproduced or transmitted in any form or by any means, electronic or mechanical, including photography, recording, or any information storage or retrieval system, without permission in writing from the publisher. The book is sold subject to the condition that it shall not, by way of trade or otherwise, be lent, resold or otherwise circulated without the publisher's prior consent in any form of binding or cover other than that in which it is published and without a similar condition, including this condition, being imposed on the subsequent purchaser.

COVER PHOTOGRAPH: "Abandoned" by David Dunn
COVER DESIGN & TYPESETTING: *Siobhán Hutson*
Printed in Ireland by Sprint Print

For M.B.

"Hope is an openness that loves your voice."
WILMER MILLS

"It's so nice to be back home where I belong."

Contents

I. *Proem*
Toils of the Road Will Then Seem as Nothing 11

II. *Start and End as One*
I'm the New Lover Helping Her Try On the Unused
    Oleg Cassini 15
Love Song 16
I Am Her Canvas 18
When I Sing for Her 19
Foxie's 21
Learning the Motions 22
Talking in My Sleep in the Northwoods 23
Where It's Shallow by the Island on Rest Lake 24
The Difference Between Tight and Loose 25
Magical Thinking 26
A Week from Wednesday 27
Coronado 28
Night Visitors 29
Tybee Still Life 31

III. *Just Tellin' It Like It Is*
I Can't Sleep with You if You Don't Like Dolly Parton ... 33
If You Ask Dolly to Take Off Her Shoes in Hawaii
    She'll Cross the Threshold on Tiptoes 34
The Reward of the Gift Waits Until Morning 36
The Picture He Took of You at Blarney Castle 38
In the Village the Night Before We Flew to Europe 39
Elitist in Central Georgia 40
Dolly and the Lolols 41

IV. I'm a Man Now, Thanks to You

Inlaid 43
I'm a One Woman Man 44
A Legend that Never Ages 45
Two Illegal U-Turns on the Way to Liberty Tattoo 46
For the Love of Dolly 47
Dolly Sees Dolly 48

V. No Rhinestone Unturned

Losing the Girl I Took to Dollywood Isn't Hard to Master . 51
Dolly Floats 53
Harmony 56
The Great Chicago Earthquake of 2002 57
Tonight Near Sunset Crater 58
Hooked 59
The Best Month for a Hand Grenade Is July 60
But You Know We Can't Live on Paint Alone 61
Ganga Aarti 62

VI. Here Is Where I'll End It

Sunday After 65
Dolly's Tour Bus Passes Through in the Middle of the Night 66
Steel Wool Inside Scratches My Lungs Apart 67
Weight 69
Did I Tell You About the Homeless Man I Saw in Riga? ... 70
Withdrawal 72
A Fitting Finale 73

Acknowledgments 74

Proem

Toils of the Road Will Then Seem as Nothing

for all who swim in the Littell gene pool

Years ago, before city water was piped up Walden Ridge
in Tennessee, water from a lake far back behind the stables
was pumped through the woods to the big house overlooking
the valley, where my grandmother's sister told us how she missed
Minnesota birch wood burning in fieldstone fireplaces.

She'd married a Nashville doctor whose hobby was pulling
the car over to take snapshots of wildflowers.
He spent many afternoons on the shoulder of the road, in a coat
and tie, belly in the grass, propped on his elbows for a close-up
of a crimson-eyed rose mallow while semis roared by.

They had more blueberries than money,
because that's what patients handed him when he delivered
their babies. In the summer we drove down from up nort'
so the whole family could picnic in the Smokies with a cranking
ice cream maker and crowd in for a picture at Rock City.
We showered our sweat and ticks off with water from their lake.

While my grandmother's sister pined for her burning
birch wood and her husband documented highway wildflowers,
they had six children. Five grew up cracking jokes like "Yankees,
go home" and prefacing legend-grand stories with "It was so funny."
Their middle son built a log cabin up the slope from the lake
with his own two hands, room by room over the years.

The zip-line that his own first-born son strung across
the lake one day was supposed to be simple enough.
It stretched from the high-reaching hickory
by the front porch of the house his daddy built
to a loblolly pine on the other side of the lake.

"Go on," this future rocket scientist was telling me
in a voice long since gentled by its darkest hour, the hour St. Jude
was 400 miles away and a miracle parted the elevator doors
to reveal a stranger with a chartered plane. "And let go
when you're halfway across the lake."

But my own heart and mind were out of balance then,
both too heavy for me to hold on to the pulley and fly
the whole way, past the rocks and stumps on the shoreline,
to the middle, where it was deepest, so he showed us how
it was done, whipped his t-shirt off, kicked his shoes off right there,
jumped up and grabbed the pulley, and with a big twang and squeak
of the rope, was on his way to the lake.

Time was kind enough to allow us to hold our breaths,
our mouths open, our eyes wide and aglow, as he swung
and he flew, bare feet skimming the flat shale in the yard,
and then over the rocks and stumps to the water, every muscle
in his shoulders taut and shiny. After he let go, his arms spread
for too short a time. The sky ran its fingers through his hair,
and then there was just a loud splash and the rope throbbing
like a loose, out-of-tune sixth string.

These days, on a hot Georgia night, the age-old pond-fossil smell
of that lake still seeps from my pores.

Start and End as One

I'm the New Lover Helping Her Try On the Unused Oleg Cassini

It's too early for certain words,
too late to recall the ones already spoken.
So says the language of sequins and floral
tulle cascading from her bodice and hem.

My hands pull and snap, hook and lift.
They are springtime curious for words
explaining now.

> A moment of clarity: at times trying to persuade
> the right word to come is simply admiring
> one's own clumsy handwriting.

Now my hands are done tugging. The last thing is to
bring her veil down over her face. And then all that's left,
while we look at both of us in the mirror,
are the tugs of reasons:

> How else to say a woman is beautiful
> without using the word beautiful?

the reasons we push away certain remembered
touches and share others, why we search
for words in a new lover's skin,
why we put fallen diamonds back into mounts.

Love Song

The slut in me tingles whenever I hear
"Whoa, come sail away with me,"

never mind I've never looked at Dolly Parton
the way most men do. Kenny must have ripped

her dress off right there in the studio, quick as shucking
corn, and now they've left us with the rest of that dynamite

melody streaming from the high ceiling,
quite a jump from the warehouse rafters

to the concrete floor, where Dolly's voice mixes
with the ink of your newest tattoo,

a red Gibson guitar wrapped in rhinestone-studded
eighth notes. A latex-gloved hand

holds your arm down, and her soprano vibrato threads
from the outline to the shading and throughout

the rest of your skin, and it knots down deep,
so deep that for the rest of your life you'll say

your blood feels like little sparrows swooping and fluttering.
From Atlanta we ride it together to Pigeon Forge,

to the new tattoo shop across from the Dollywood
Express, a hop, skip, and a jump from the Village

Carousel, where no one heeds the warning of addiction.
The artist there tells you the three Dolly choices

are top sellers: Here-You-Come-Again Dolly,
Coat-of-Many-Colors Dolly, or Rainbow Dolly,

but he doesn't decline to do an old-school
mermaid on your other forearm and a pair of claws

around your elbow for your eventual nautical sleeve.
Raw and swollen and glaring, a pile of cotton candy

and a funnel cake later, plus a sinful deep-fried Snickers
on a stick, we're bone-sore on the tram through the parking lot

back to the car. A little boy next to us points to the face
of the mermaid. It is the face of Dolly, beauty spot and all.

After dark, when I put my head on your chest, I hear her
singing in your heartbeat. I think she is singing to me.

I Am Her Canvas

She starts with the silvergray signature logo from
Here You Come Again on my left forearm
and three Ed Caraeff Dolly Partons in red
tie waist shirts and bell bottom jeans
on my right shoulder. She grows my hair out
and colors it black, keeps me on a diet
until I fit in skinnies, finds me the perfect
high-top Converse kicks, stresses the leather
of my new bomber jacket so it looks vintage,
moves me into a loft in Cabbagetown, where she hangs
a Dolly poster above the headboard and it changes poses,
smiles, outfits, because something in the ink
is breathing. Some days her tiger eyes tat bleeds
brighter colors. Some days it shrinks and retreats
behind the curtains of her veins. Some nights
just two lacy red bra straps float it to her skin
like a face behind her reflected in the melted wax
of tealights. These are the nights
my new ones are most brilliant.

When I Sing for Her

Not too long ago I said I'd do anything for her
except sing. But that was then and this is now.

Now, love is the whole bakery.
Then, infatuation was the stripper

in the cake. Sooner or later we grow
tired of pasties and licking the frosting off

our fingers, so
today her grandmother's china

plates are stacked in
my cupboard. Our toothbrushes

touch in the bathroom. Two packs
a day for a few weeks

and I am ready, voice
so buried in grit and cinders the paint

goes wet and the hardwood
floors buckle when I crack

the Dolly, Linda, and Emmylou
version of "Rosewood Casket." Fleas

from the previous tenants leap
from the chips in the floorboards.

Neighbors come out looking around.
My grandmother always said,

"A joyful noise, clear and loud," which was half-baked
advice for a no-audience kind of guy like me

who cringed under the whole-bakery voice
my grandmother saved purely for Sacred

Heart and Father Goodhead,
but who now lets his own fly like buckshot

tearing apart her sheer curtains.
I can close my eyes and I hear Grandma now,

shrill like metalworking, on tiptoes for the high
notes, her Kleenex-dust mustache

gray as leaf-pile smoke
above a grove of bare sweetgums.

When a song ends in an empty room,
the unsung overture is, "I love you, please."

Foxie's

It closed years
ago. Summer customers
couldn't find it at the end
of this pinecone-peppered road
down the woods. We whisper
about the Ramble's black tupelo at Central
Park, where the moon was a marshmallow
on a stick like tonight, step cautiously
up the broken steps in
front, pull apart the rusty
padlock that no longer locks.
This is our best secret.
Inside we open our journal with blank
pages, struggle to plant stories
in it together. The white
sheets imply it's time
to let out the breath we've held.
Nothing comes to us
except the moonlight through
a crack in the ceiling above
the bar. Bottles empty and filled
with cobwebs snaring dust
suggest a memory sets better
than what might come.
For now we pretend to be
carefree, like Foxie herself these days
when she checks her mailbox and finds
nothing in it.

Learning the Motions

The winter we had no snow she taught me
to skate. The ice across the bay past the island
closest to our cottage was just thick enough to hold
us two. We left our gloves and jackets inside. She pulled
me along behind her, said "You're my Radio
Flyer!" until I let go and wobbled off, my knees
locked and ankles flopping.

I wasn't sure how to love
that woman who squeaked when
I went down, hands out to catch my
slip. But then she lay next to me. Together
we licked the ice, tasted the solder
of the lake, asked each other what shapes we saw
in the cast-iron, catfish-gray water underneath.

When we lost the feeling
under our sweaters, in our faces and fingers, we went inside to
flannel pajamas and blackberry toddies. Into the evening
we still felt fringes of wind curling around us,
we never guessed how close we'd come to breaking through.

Talking in My Sleep in the Northwoods

We weren't supposed to be in the same room.
I don't remember any of my dreams, but

she watched me sleep all night and pried
them open like wispy cocoons. I tossed and

turned on the floor, blanket twisted around
my legs. She rocked in the wooden chair

by the front windows, her foot on the corner
of my pillow. She hummed the song we'd made

up on the warped piano at home downstairs.
I was alert enough to see some things:

The sky was so sharp the stars were sharks'
teeth. Winterghosts from the island across the lake

came moon-tickled out of their hiding places looking
like milky blemishes on weathered varnish.

They listened outside the frosted windows to the rocker's
snreeck-snreeck, her humming browned by bourbon,

and the German phrases I slurred, a honeyed harmony.
Like us, they left no tracks in the snow.

Where It's Shallow by the Island on Rest Lake

We never decided on a name
for the island that wasn't always
an island. When the lake was
spilled out into the woods, first
half a hill was carved away like a butternut
husk. Its north side was left
a cliff, abrupt and chopped,
and slippery furrows steeply channeled straight
down into the water. We came in close, steered
our pedal boat over submerged box
springs, porcelain basins and pitchers, the jagged triangle
of a mirror that reflected itself in the water reflection
of our faces. We might have reached in
and grabbed it all to keep, but to us it
seemed guarded a hundred feet under.
And who's to say the surface wouldn't slice
through our arms at the elbows and keep them
detached and preserved from us, specimens suspended
like gruesome swizzle sticks?
Once I whispered out the front
windows at the night blotted island
for it to haunt me. I wanted to wizard blast
the bulldozed cabin back together, summon
its people to return so I could cry *You never knew*
the twisted operatic flare of your bedroom
mirror until this lake reached in.

The Difference Between Tight and Loose

Everywhere she goes she carries a built-in saloon.
The first time you see her in *Best Little Whorehouse*
she comes down the Chicken Ranch staircase to a rinky-tink
piano, only it's not a piano—it's just the little bitty pissant
rhinestones jingling on her apple-peel dress. The moment
Colin Higgins yelled "Action!" while filming that scene
in Texas, I was seven and skipped the school bus in Monona
to walk home from Immaculate Heart of Mary with Jon Marks.
We were cocksure we'd beat the bus, and our mothers
would never know. We stopped by Kenna Ringo's and rang her
doorbell for plums off her tree. Juice sticky
on our chins, we talked of Mrs. Moriarity always
driving forty miles an hour, because "Mrs. Moriarity"
and "forty miles an hour" were the first words we loved
repeating. Meanwhile, guess whose mothers were worrying
at the bus stop up the hill from Birch Haven Circle.
Once in a while Dolly says James Woods is a great kisser.
There's straight talk for you. The same time she shot
that scene in Chicago I was seventeen in Manitowish Waters
grilling on a pontoon with a dark-haired girl, anchored
by an island with a gingerbread house. Don't ask her name—
I only remember she was on the water ski team
and untied the top of her black bikini when the moon
was full enough to light up her shoulders.

Magical Thinking

for Graham Lorenzo

Songwriters like Dolly Parton are born with all the songs
they'll ever write. This is to say that, to a baby,
language is a white horse in the night
under a bare pecan tree, as blurred
as a forgotten dream remembered only now.

But look what happens when the baby's mother reads
him Joan Didion in fading light. Imagine we're
inside his head, where surely lamplight and sunsetlight
must filter through delicate, paper-thin canvas of the tent
that skin makes—all the words he'll ever learn
before the sorrow of past tense, before ink
is blurred by rain, are gathered already,
their arms raised, shouting a revival
for those carried by his mother's voice.

There's no shame in feeding each other
like we're babies—the only shame is the impossibility
of using all words or singing all songs
of a lifetime at once.

Someday the baby will see the sky on a night
so clear and dark he can tell which stars
are farther away than others, and words
return to white horses galloping up the hill.

A Week from Wednesday

I have no choice but to bury the baby swift.
It must have been searching for a Dolly song
to go to during the storm last night.
It survived the nest fall only to die by itself,
crying—beak open, eyes closed—with no sound.

Soon you'll leave for a month.
What I remember most about Île Saint-Louis
are the crisscrossed double shadows I cast
on the bridges. If you truly come back you'll uncork
your last Picchetti Mission Anjelica
and wistfully recall two sets of them.

Suppose I tell you don't go.
A time may come when you request the same
of me. My heart bronzed in
wanderlust may not be able to stay either.

We could have had this conversation
after soaking up the white primer
we spilled on the gray carpet by the sofa,
but instead we dipped strawberries in chocolate
and blew trumpets with sugar-coated lips.

Coronado

I find a panda lunch
      pail washed ashore. It seems a boy

         who wanted to be a surfer instead of
a fisherman was dragging it alongside his
      father's boat until he let go.

         The pail is dented and metal,
a kinked coil of line tied to the handle.

      If I had the magic to do so I'd scoop up the whole sea, all the way
         past the horizon and then some, and lug the pail
overflowing with tides to The Del,

      where I'd pour the water flecked
         with disturbed shipwrecks and eels into a pyramid

crystal pendant so that you can carry all
      the oceans of the world around your neck.

Night Visitors

That dreadful holiday when no one knew what
to do with me, she invited herself over for White
Christmas and Merlot and ended up spending
the night after my 2:00 in the morning slurred
requests to toast ourselves again next year.
She raised her glass and spoke with hairline cracks
in the engraved bookends holding up her words.

I slipped out of bed quietly to pace off the wine
dreams. I plugged in the lights wrapped around
my living room lamp shade, an improvised tree
in a moment of unexpected but thoroughly welcome
company. I threw away some scrunched Frosty
and Rudolph wrapping paper left on the floor.

I spent a few minutes watching her through the dark,
got in bed with her quietly once more, stared at the ceiling.
This wasn't routine enough for sleep to come easily, so
an old family memory played in my head:

My father and step-mother, both relaxed
on their bed together one color-tinted Saturday morning,
pointing out to each other animal crackers and critter
faces they were seeing in the knotted pine-planked
and varnished cathedral ceiling of their bedroom.
"An otter," my dad said. "A koala," my step-mother said.
"A raccoon!" "No, a manatee!" "Look, there's a dolphin!"

When she drove off before sunrise, I went back to bed
on the side she'd slept on. I fell asleep blanketed
in the purr of her cigarette scent and the meandering
garlands of the French perfume I forgot to ask the name of.
I felt myself flip and glide in an ocean warm
and liquored with swimmers and dolphins
bullying away the blacktips with their bottlenoses.

Tybee Still Life

The silver rolo chain long and diagonal
across her breast, pulled tight and hooked

in her thumb, her ginger hair a fan
across the ivory sheet, she floats

for him in bed like the young martyr in water.
Bees, not wind, outside the window

pull the ropes to the silent white carillon
petals on three Carolina Silverbells.

Also three butterflies, each
the monarch of its own campanile.

He should remember all of this,
should listen to her tell how far

it feels between now and next time,
but he's left with just new stars,

so visible here a pier-length past the edge
of the country the constellations

blend in among them. He even forgets
her pillowcase on the line overnight.

When he gathers it just before daybreak,
holds it to his face before folding,

it smells like the sweat between the legs
of Georgia ghosts. They pass coldly through

the black widow far back behind
Battery Garland to spread her moans.

Just Tellin' It Like It Is

I Can't Sleep with You if You Don't Like Dolly Parton

Pretend this is
a pay-what-you-think-is-fair
restaurant. You can find places
like this if you know
where to look. No
lie. A pickle jar full of
money protects innocent
and guilty, only in our case
we're talking
about your fightin' words.
Maybe some folks are broke,
maybe some leave two twenties
for a glass of rosewater
lemonade and a lunch plate
of falafel, but I love it
I'm the cheap one here,
the one who buttons up fast and runs
out while the dime still tinkles
because you, the baklava,
were too tart instead of sweet.

If You Ask Dolly to Take Off Her Shoes in Hawaii She'll Cross the Threshold on Tiptoes

Back home I love only one habit
I can't break, and for her I might
buy a pareo, so the dark-eyed pareo
girl in the open-air lobby
of my resort on the windward side
of the Big Island sells me one
while the complimentary shuttle train
clatters along the canal past the concierge.
A long time ago at Dollywood,
I saw Dolly Parton in a floral-lei pareo,
but it wasn't genuine, for it had sleeves.
Dolly calypso-paraded out from backstage
at the Pines Theatre to sing a song
with pannists from Trinidad and Tobago,
who were there for the Festival of Nations,
far, far away from any real country.
The pareo girl shows me all the ways
you can wrap and tie an aquamarine
demonstration pareo. The tropic breath
of the Pacific blows it around her
surf-toned legs holding sway over me.
The boat ferrying check-ins
moors up near us. Airplane-exhausted
wives clomp aboard in high heels
while their husbands in polo shirts
steady them with one hand and tip
the bellhop with the other.
Did you know Dolly Parton
has balanced on stilettos for so long
she can no longer walk flatfooted, that
she has rubber heels for the shower?

A retired golden-ager from Arizona stops
to comment on the pareo I want,
because it's her first Hawaii
experience and she's ready
for the luau. Me and the pareo girl
pose with the lady's sky-high silver
hair and desert-rock skin.
This seems as inauthentic as my first time
in Paris, when Japanese tourists on top
of the Arc de Triomphe thought
I was French and pulled me into
all their pictures. Maybe I'll go
to Japan someday and discover myself
in a framed photo above a rice cooker.
Anyway, when the pareo girl finishes
showing Lagoon Pagoda spenders
all the ways of wrapping and tying
pareos, she meets me on the lava-rock
beach to swing in a hammock strung
between coconut palms. And guess
what? She says a year or so ago
she tied a pareo for Dolly.
My new leeward life—
papayas, mangoes, and pareos.

The Reward of the Gift
Waits Until Morning

I don't know if I should put on the Irish
wool socks she's given me upon her flaring return

from three months away on the other side of the ocean.
I had no idea she'd bring back the ordinary.

When she falls asleep I trace the veins in my foot.
They've recently risen after dropping their weights

in the wells of my blood. Were they pressured
up to the surface by days and days of walking

on cobblestone thousands of miles from here, back when
I about died to pose cultured and cosmopolitan?

This purple spirograph flower below my right
malleolus bone blooms, proof of a motorcycle skid.

And here's the toenail that still grows crooked and cracked
a year after a bare crushing blow from a dropped car battery,

and this bump that shouldn't be might be the navicular bone
that healed out of place after I slipped on icy doorsteps.

I learned long ago that a quarter of the body's bones
are in the feet and ankles. As if looking for a secret,

I pull at my two middle toes connected at
the middle joint by a flap of extra flesh.

In the morning, her temple is glazed from a twist of my sleep
tears or whatever watery words I might have mumbled

while calling for the secrets and unseen defects
also rolled up in the scrolls of her own skin.

The Picture He Took of You at Blarney Castle

There you are in the tower
on the way down. I should be
the reason for that smile,
that learned pose with one sandal
crossed behind the other, that love
song you are jotting notes
for behind your eyes.
*Je n'ai pas fait un bisou
sur la roche*, you will write me
tomorrow on a Guinness postcard,
Je parle bien déjà!
You stand on uneven stone
steps, faux Gucci bag over
your shoulder. Your slender
fingers rest on the steel
railing polished clean
by thousands of careful
hands before you. Look
closely and you'll see
your fingers trembling.
Have you ever noticed
a leaf fall, only to be cradled
up again by the wind so
it snagged among leaves
still on branches and hung
just a little while longer?
You might see it tremble too.
It knows each tiny movement
brings it closer to falling one
last time. *Mais oui*, I will agree
silently, *N'est-ce pas?*

In the Village the Night Before We Flew to Europe

we danced the Yellow
Brick Road Off to See
the Wizard song arm
in arm in the dusk
rain, she in strappy
sandals and me in hemp
flip flops kicking
up puddles just as easy
and fast as a bike
with no fenders.
Our sprinkler children
toes splashed and played
right down to it while the
people in the lit from inside boat
size windows of a Mediterranean
restaurant clinked their
Malmsey in olive tree
stem glasses.
Somehow we stayed
upright, like the guitar
case in the corner
of my bathroom,
buckles rusty after four
Sundays absorbing love
steam from hour long
morning after showers—
A year of nightfalls spent
drowning the funny way
you brushed the hair out of
my eyes couldn't polish them clean.
Anyone would have thought
we'd stumble, but our legs
were plumb banjo
strings tuning to the cycles
that we live over
and over again regardless.

Elitist in Central Georgia

Now terrorists can blow up airplanes with regular-size deodorant,
shaving cream, and toothpaste, which requires a crawl through a traffic jam
of deluxe-cab pick-ups to the local big-box store for travel-size ones.
In the parking lot a black Lincoln is in the way, waiting for
a handicapped spot occupied by a yellow Volkswagen convertible.
Lincoln thinks Volkswagen is backing out, but the top just goes
up and down, up and down. Dixie horns toot.
Middle fingers salute from rolled-down windows.
Inside, rednecks and Baptists all over. The sheriff's wife,
her wig crooked, abandons her cart and purse in the aisle to read
moisturizer labels. "Bless your heart," she says.
Girls cutting school flip through Hannah Montana posters.
Prefer Miley's Aunt Dolly myself.
At the self checkout I push the Spanish button, for fun.
A big & jiggly jellyroll man wearing a greasy trucker cap coasts his electric
cart to a stop. He says I should learn English or get
the hell out of the country. His sweat pants and flannel shirt
haven't been off him in days. You have no idea how much I hate
dirty white socks and fat ankles. I tell him to piss off in German.

Dolly and the Lolols

For Liz

Tweeters haven't figured out how to make a laugh
look real. A capital LOL is stupid. I don't believe
it's a belly roll, can't imagine LollyLips82
shrieking so hard she's crying. You're the only one
I know who has never once used lol. This is why
I welcome your hahas. They are literal, gutsy, vintage
like the heels of your cowboy boots tocking louder
up the hall. A good laugh doesn't fit in any abbreviation.
Remember when Dolly was on an awards show
and her dress split open? I doubt she likes texting
because it must be hard with those long nails,
and how would she pack her laugh into three tiny letters?
Well, maybe four if she drawls it out like this: lawl.
It's still fifty pounds of mud in a five-pound bag,
bowling balls in a marble sack.

I'm a Man Now, Thanks to You

Inlaid

All of us are born with invisible coloring-book
lines. Our bodies know where tattoos will
someday be outlined and shaded, like
my eyes always knew they'd see the Taj Mahal.
This explains why, in Agra last summer, I choked up
and let tears come behind my sunglasses. A heart knows
who it will fall in love with years before it breaks.
A songwriter knows her song before it's finished.
The never-felt-before sting of Dolly
surfacing in lines and shades on my baby-shaved
forearm is familiar, like a marble dome
and reflecting pools at dawn. The watermarks
elsewhere on my body itch for future definition:
an Eiffel Tower on my ankle, Dolly's signature
logo on my wrist, a microphone stand and tragedy/comedy
masks on the other forearm, the Taj Mahal
somewhere undetermined, floating unanchored.

I'm a One Woman Man

A real, live Dolly was inked
on my forearm last Wednesday on Ponce

in Atlanta around midnight in a little tattoo
parlor full of crucifixes and Virgin Marys.

Today she's flaking while she heals,
like she's recuperating from plastic surgery,

only tattoo recovery isn't considered a valid
excuse for sick leave. She is forced to go to work

with me and put up with everyone touching
and taking pictures of her ugly, raw, chemical-peel

face. She is suffocating under lotion, struggling
down there for air, dying to sing "Together You and I."

A Legend that Never Ages

A few days after the bloody,
oozy vernix has washed off, the Dolly
tattoo on my forearm bubbles
when she gets wet in the shower
or cleansed with gentle, sensitive-skin
Dove. Cloudy smears of baby
lotion blur her details. She starts to peel
as she dries overnight when I'm asleep,
leaves in my sheets salt-and-pepper trails
of paper-skin flakes furrowed with black ink.
Because she's my first, I just about have a heart
attack when it looks as if her eyelash
has scuttled away—I toss and turn all night
worrying her hair will go flat. What if her breasts
sag and deflate? Can a broken high heel be glued?
Soon comes the moment, like ice
falling off a tree after the sun finally
warms what's left of a winter storm, when she sings me
a little song she made up about plastic surgery.
Take it from her, she says, healing
requires composure. Even then, who is
ever satisfied? So thanks
to several more mornings of patting
lotion on her, Dolly shines tight
once again. Before long she bats her eyelashes
fresh and pretty. Her cleavage points
plump and perky. Her teeth
sparkle and ting. She glows the way
she burned for the spotlight
on the day she was born.

Two Illegal U-Turns on the Way to Liberty Tattoo

I thought she might be immortal there,
but, like holy water, wooden stakes, and garlic,
the new Dolly tattoo on my forearm
fears a few things:

Mailboxes. Specifically, when I wave her
out the window of a speeding Lexus
and you curve too close to one.
Who's to say the doctor will care
to set her correctly after a break like that?

Copperheads. A bite to the wrist
and she'll swell up like a swampy
balloon and split open between her breasts,
then get covered by a meshed graft that looks,
ironically, like snake skin.

The song in the ink. It's a good one,
about you and me pulled over on the highway
to Atlanta, the five shots you slammed
at the bar next door while the needles
drill-scored the clef, time signature, and staff
of our sheet music permanently into me.

But Dolly knows all good songs arrive
at the last vibrato note, all travelers
choose a new way. She worries
I'll grow woebegone of her
singing our song forever.

For the Love of Dolly

The two girls in California who dug
Dolly's used Q-tips and Nippits
from her trash and put them on
display in a booth at the next year's collector
convention might be the same
girls who bought a Honda once driven
by Dolly's personal assistant. It ain't worth
remembering who's who, only that they squealed
when they found a long blonde hair
in the front seat, and licked the seat belts
for traces of perfume. Someday I will meet Dolly
and show her the Dolly tattoo on my arm.
Maybe it will be as awkward as a best friend
telling her he's in love with her, unless Dolly strokes it
with her fingernail and starts humming notes to herself.
Either way, I will let Dolly know it has nothing to do
with her, that I was curious about pain, but not mine,
which is just an apple with a bite out of it
I found on my lawn yesterday. It's possible
to not get enough of someone else's.
It's like the closer you are to the sky
the bigger it seems. If you look at my redhead
inamorata, a foxy, easy-on-the-eye
killer in her fedora, leather jacket,
and black cowboy boots, you can't help
wondering how much those sixteen
tattoos of her own must have hurt,
whether or not she interrupts living
to feel what a little bit of dying
might be like. And now I'm addicted.

Dolly Sees Dolly

for Liz, who was there when it happened

At the Sevier County High School graduation in 1964,
a young Dolly Rebecca Parton announced she was boarding
the bus to Nashville the next morning to be a star.
The laughter that volleyed off the shiny basketball
floor and the rows of fidgety-hard chairs was the same
she'd heard for her coat of many colors years back.
Imagine the silence from that crowd of nonbelievers
if she'd said, "Someday at my theme park, maybe in 2011,
a fan will show me his tattoo of me."

So let's talk about that Dolly tattoo getting inked.
The first thing it sang to me in healing, when the flaky
skin around her mouth fell away a few days later,
was, "He's got a wandering eye and a traveling mind,
big ideas and a little behind." How funny when things
we've always known become known.

See how the stars stay where they are
when you drive as fast as you can down the country.
Relatively speaking, we aren't moving at all,
but the wind in our hair and the telephone poles casting power
lines hearsay otherwise. The signs in the headlights
bring Memphis closer by the hour, but what if
it never gets to us because we have to turn off 200
miles before? What if all you & I can be is a highway
under a star that gets it in its mind to bust loose and leap,
like a rhinestone falling off a black cocktail dress?

This is the real Dolly, driven in her Dewitt antique
car, waving at all who've come to Dollywood.

In the moment of eye contact, the Dolly cartoonized
on my right arm from elbow to wrist flares hot,
tingles green and yellow, balloons life-size and more,
flames in full Dollyized make-up color, hair teased,
lips red as two ruts through a wet Georgia
junkyard, puff of smoke and flashing spotlights,
neon pink signature logo a glow-stick butterfly
looping in the air around you & me.

You might could describe it as an explosion.

If we were a little closer to the Dolly in the car,
we'd see her powder floating in bubbling foundation,
mascara running, real hair singed under her wig.
Our own faces are blackened, our own hair
scorched and blown. Out of thousands in the crowd,
it's just us three burned like that.

As soon as she rolls by
and keeps riding along the ticker-tape
route through her park,
the ink in my arm suddenly cools,
dries and settles,
only the smile looks
a little pouty now.

No Rhinestone Unturned

Losing the Girl I Took to Dollywood
Isn't Hard to Master

So why did I go to the wedding
under the Burke Brise Soleil last Saturday?
Because forgetting is like the clouds
moving toward the horizon. Once one
is gone, another comes after
in a different shape.
Which brings me back

to Dollywood. Right there,
around the corner
from the Southern Gospel
Museum and Hall of Fame, inhale
as long and hard as you can.
The last time I brought her here
some smoke from one of her American
Spirits wrapped around the leaves
in a haze and stuck around for my coming again.
Draw it down so it enters your lungs once more.
It tastes as unsettling as the realization
that the last time I'd seen the bride
was two years ago when she left
my flat in Riverwest early in the morning.
Which brings me back

to Dollywood. I return
because I have stared at an empty wallet
when I needed a bottle of Evan Williams
and a pack of Camels, and because I have
woken up in the night with my hand
on the pillow next to me, dream-tricked
into thinking it was her back.
Which brings me back

to Dollywood, because these days I drive
through the part of town wiped out
by a tornado—trees snapped in half,
gas station twisted and uprooted,
church roof peeled down to the timber
trusses—without noticing anything
out of the ordinary. And because
lately only a tequila-logged fire ant
struggling on the rim of my cactus-stem
margarita glass has given my lip a sting.

Dolly Floats

2004

The American flag Dolly rode on
was hard to tell apart from her dress.
They put her in a plastic box like the Pope
to protect her from the bullets
of a cold front. The next morning Dolly,
as an Irish peasant girl, blew a penny
whistle, then she was rushed over to Jukebox
Junction where, in a red-silk skirt
and spiky wig, she took the stage
with Chinese acrobats throwing plates.

2005

Again the Pope box from last year to keep
Dolly dry in her foresty Friday-night-parade
dress. For Dollywood's 20th anniversary
she cooked up a cake-candles-and-presents float.
Saturday Mardi Gras at Dollywood cancelled
on account of a steely, stationary rain,
so no strutting her peacock feathers for Dolly,
no mask, no butterfly wand, no stilt walkers.

2006

Damsel-in-distress Dolly lashed to a log
getting sawed in a great whirling blade.
A lumberjack chopped her ropes
and freed her so she could launch Timber
Canyon at Dollywood and spread the curtains
at the new Sweet Shoppe on Showstreet.
Dolly spun a purple parasol and
cut the taffy ribbon.

2007

Dolly the leprechaun roosted golden in a pot
at the end of a rainbow float.
I don't remember much because the Applejacks
at the Night of 1000 Dollies party
in Knoxville were strong.
Dolly's brother and sister showed up,
as did her niece, who sang some songs,
along with a whole gaggle of drag
queens preening in their Dolly.

2008

Dolly and her Huckleberry-Finn bluejean
capris braved a raft on the edge of a plaster
waterfall. I skipped Dolly's Nudie
& the Wagonmasters tribute
to Porter, because I saw him
at the Opry House a year ago in his last
televised performance with her.

2009

Dolly tipped her ranger hat to Smokey
Bear and climbed a ladder to a straight
back chair in a ranger station on wheels
pulled by a pick-up. A few hours before,
she was awarded an honorary doctorate
from the University of Tennessee, so now
she'll be forever known as Dr. Double-D.

2010

I missed Dolly
as grand marshall, because I bought
a ticket to India without checking the dates.
I was in Varanasi waiting for the lights
to come back on and watching bodies
burn on the banks of the Ganges.
According to the pictures I saw,
Dolly wore an aluminum-foil pixie
get-up and her float was a wedding
cake. Or a battleship.

2011

Dolly walked the wings of a bi-plane
float in boots with heels so high
we thought she'd fall.
She tossed her scarf over her shoulder.
The only time we saw her eyes
was when she took off her bomber
glasses just once.

Harmony

The south
side of town,
a hole-in-the-wall
cantina no white
guy except me is aware
of, in the middle of a gang
grid. The bartender
already knows you want
a margarita on the rocks.
With salt. So no need
to order one. Catarina
in a china poblana fans out
from the cocina with
a plate of arroz
con papas y guisantes
because they're your favorite.
I took Dolly there last time
she passed through.
The five minutes
she sang "Jolene"
with the mariachi trumpets
and guitarron
were worth the gunshots
at the stoplight
on the way. Their Spanish
lyrics and her English
lyrics braided together
in the guacamole
molcajete.

The Great Chicago Earthquake of 2002

The ghost of Mrs. O'Leary's cow spared the House of Blues
the night Dolly Parton teetered into that toddlin' town
in her pointed-toe mules with mile-high heels. She sang & picked
stripped-down bluegrass for gay standing-room-only
packed-to-overflowing city slickers. One flame too close
to her wig when she bent down to grab some roses
and the whole place could have gone up in explosions
gamboling from beer breath to beer breath,
cologne boa to cologne boa.
It was as far as you could get from the back porch
on Locust Ridge in Tennessee, where stamping feet
rumbled a hundred miles through ancient shale
and blue smoke all the way from the Mountain Opry
to her old autoharp and wooden chair rocking over the valley.
I was there in the stormy, husky, brawling freight handler
of the nation when it happened, when she plucked a stray
platinum hair dangling over her eye. The music slowed down
and high notes lowered to bass while it floated to her feet.
When it hit the floor of the stage she kept right on sailing
through "After the Goldrush," same speed as before.
Seismologists were puzzled the world over when
the corncob towers of Marina City swayed so much
they touched their tops. Long after the aftershock music
ended, and she was back in her custom purple Prevost
heading south, it was determined Dearborn was the unheard-of
epicenter. A shuffling janitor with a wide broom swept
that single hair into a dust bin.

Tonight Near Sunset Crater

I give her salt on her tongue, tequila
all the way down to her toes, ice between
her teeth, crushed like sugar rocks.

This rocky state has something to hide
from us after twilight. Cabochon
birds settle under rabbitbrush.
Gemstone peaks turn rough
and dull before the morning
facets them again.

For now the only
chatoyancy left is an island
of aspens by the trail, where
together we pick up a bleeding
Spotted Sandpiper.

From under its wing I tweeze a fish
hook. She quickly dabs the wound
with a fingertip of alcohol before
the orange-billed feather storm in our hands
flips and forces us to let go,

to watch it in our stupors
take bow-winged fluttery flight
over the cinder-strewn slopes
we've come so far to appraise.

Hooked

The woman on the boat
is grilling crab cakes.
She gives one to the man skippering.
He takes only a careful, tentative bite.
Then they're in the lock
before Lake Mendota.
It won't open. They're left to go
up and down
up and down
as the water rises and lowers.
Again. Again.

A boy chisels a heart in a tree.
A girl feeds bread to a mallard drake.

And here's how I feel about this.
I'd rather drive you up a mountain
highway at midnight,
squeal around blind hairpin turns,
cross the center line, look out
the sunroof and watch
the star-splattered sky reel
left and right faster than the moon
swings back and forth through our lives.

But there's nothing to do now except wait
for the lock to unstick or let the boat
slowly spin in the eddy.

The Best Month for a Hand Grenade Is July

Too many Tropical Itches
and Horny Gators reveal the cop
by the door goes commando under his uniform.
Wildman Eric is the name on his badge.
Someone has left behind some Vouvray
chenin blanc on the urinal in a green bottle
smudged with lipstick and fingerprints.
A walking-tour ghost who has the night off
gives it a swirl. My forehead on the wall
slows the spinning. Dolly catches me,
parts my hair with the rubies
in her fingernails, cradles my head on the cherry
guipure of her stay-up that the slit of her red
dress is high enough to show, raises me to my feet
with "House of the Rising Sun." A buck a spank
rakes in enough for carriage fare from the Funky Pirate
to Bootleggers to the Maison Rouge, where,
in the morning, we ask Wildman Eric to leave
because of a smell. I don't see anything dead
under the bed, just a drain through which all this
glorious city spirals down to the roots of the steaming
hot muskeg it was built on.

But You Know We Can't
Live on Paint Alone

I hope Dolly Parton once in a while
lets someone do her make-up
the way we splatter paint on each other.

First, red flung across our faces,
then purple flicked on our foreheads.
Up and down and across our necks and shoulders,

green becomes suede fringe windblown
in these shutter-house shadows stirred by the ceiling fan.
Black is mascara smeared on our cheeks

as if we are playing dress-up before a vanity
and missing our eyelashes on account of all this
laughing, Belle the chow-collie

barking and stepping in circles,
a spilled rainbow of paw prints on the hardwood.
White is a bare-arm sleeve of rhinestones.

When we're done, yellow is both a highlight
and undertone of sticky, drippy wigs.
A sloppy Dolly is the best Dolly

we can be for ourselves,
but even Dolly might agree the greatest
trust is a splattered one, because coloring outside

our lines is when we care enough to look
our very most beautiful best.

Will you cut my hair now?

Ganga Aarti

*Benares is older than history, older than tradition,
    older even than legend, and looks twice as old as all
        of them put together.*
                                            MARK TWAIN

I meet Dolly at the river of light and
water buffalo, sacred morning baths,
cobras in baskets, temples, pyres,
burning bodies. Piled up in high daytime
on Dasaswamedh Ghat, sandalwood-infused
heat unfurls now at sunset from the dust,
a reliable, smoky, ashy, jet lag tonic.

It is the incensed puja that raises her on a pillar
of light between two wooden boats
rickety with tourists setting flower bowls
afloat, adrift. Leis of wick lamps drop
from Dolly's sleeves and trail like fringe.

Dry as talcum powder,
a wake of cleansed and purified
water silvering behind her,
she wades aground up the stone steps,
where bindi hawkers,
saffron-robed pandits, and holy
sadhus clear a path of stares.

At the platform, under clanging cymbals,
she regards me watching her from a sari
shop balcony, and this is what she says:

"Hello, Stephen."

Here Is Where I'll End It

Sunday After

If I could misplace a single morning
it would be this one.

Here even the dust echoes
almost as loud as the bath
faucet dripping since last month. She gathered
her purse, lipstick, belt, shoes,
and key ring with its plastic monkey
wearing a yellow beret. That was an hour ago.

Down the porch steps she left because
she had trouble sleeping. To tell
you the truth, so did I.
Maybe I knew she'd only
peek in the front windows
of this guest cottage in my heart. She won't settle in,
claim the unlocked china cabinets, sleepwalk the nicked
hardwood hallways, or hang her coat
on the wobbly hook, dribbling plaster,
over the radiator.

Where can I fold up
and put away today's
morning, so vast and wide the falling tablecloth
in my chest cannot settle over it all?

Dolly's Tour Bus Passes Through in the Middle of the Night

during the dark summer
of empty baseball diamonds,
vodka splashed on capelli d'angelo pasta,
Cadillacs and Mercurys parked at the drive-in
under story light flickering through mosquito clouds.

Only words come when you no longer do,
memorized, sleep-sung softly
to made-up melody, to myself,
hand under your word-song breast.

Morning, the dustprints
of every word on the hardwood
follow the door, the elderberry dream
of the past perfect
inveterate deep in their letterbones.

Steel Wool Inside Scratches
My Lungs Apart

Too many Camels on the front
porch bring the sun down faster.

I hear the past is in those stars. Imagine
ten-million-year-old light, still
fast as the day it was born, loaded
with panoramas from a yellow dwarf
and its planets that might not shine
or orbit anymore. Can it be calculated
where I must launch myself to see the light
from Earth that carries the way
things were, before all this,
like an unopened letter
about bad haircuts and old dogs?

Suppose it were possible to haul
a telescope up past the belt of Orion,
sometimes called the Three Marys,
which I prefer, and focus on the good
earthlight of early memories.
I might have described to you my first
one. All I remember is I had a headache
and wanted a Band-Aid for my forehead.

Jump to Mother's Day
twenty-some years ago. My brother washed
my step-mother's car with S.O.S. pads.
He meant well. My heart too is steel
wool wrapped around gossamer.

Regardless, the idea of distant space
travel is fruitless,

because somewhere out there
the lights from the stars go out.
That's not mentioning new
stars with light we can't yet see.
So how would celestial navigation ever
work for going somewhere farther than here?
These purpling fingers of mine have no choice
but to redraw the maps
of the heavens with expanses
dark as Faulkner's eyes.

But stare Faulkner down long enough
and he pulls you into a flickering-light
corridor where a lifetime of breathing
is wheezed to only this: a Partonian voice
on a T.V. behind a closed door admits
sunny Dolly once faced a decision to shoot
her brains out or get off her fat butt.

A blind tuxedo cat licks herself in the leaves.
I'm not a cat person. I'd rather have your headlights
swinging through the low-hanging branches
at the end of the driveway.

Just as the night starts to fold in
totally white, quarters forgotten in a pocket
clink in the spin cycle. Last week,
when I hoped my plane back would crash
and you said it was a terrible thing
to say, for then what would you do,
I daydreamed those coins rolling and bouncing
through fire across the tarmac.

The code in their rattling
gathers me to the keys on the counter.

Weight

When I learned *all* matter has gravity, I refused to believe.
It explained why pewter-framed London photos stayed,
and scuffed red dancing shoes far back in the closet,
antique tea kettles boxed up from house to house,
but didn't explain the loss of hubcaps,
olive oil bottles taken by the ex,
a son across town who hasn't called in seven years.
Searching in the basement for a glass-topped table unseen
since moving in, I find folders of yellowed French and German
essays written in college, held together with rusted staples
and words I forgot I knew, meanings long gone.
Words outlast those who wrote them.
That's the beauty in Christmas Eve
suicides of poets, and so is listening
hard for weakening echoes of last ones whispered.
Every story we've made survives this broken life,
deep-rooted in grace of their own,
until their margins wear down like a statue carved in reverse,
reverting to a block of marble.
Cleaning is how I get trapped.
Barefoot on a chair, leaning on tiptoes,
dusting the top of the cabinet.
Three crystal wine goblets with hand-painted mountains
shatter on the ceramic tile floor and spread
a blanket of shards and peaks.
What am I to do but believe now?
Away down the street papers with foreign words I once typed,
accents added in pencil, sail like children
because the trash collectors are careless and gravity
doesn't exist.

Did I Tell You About the Homeless Man I Saw in Riga?

You stole my feather
boa valentine candies,
punctured my rubber
cushion with a rusted nail bent
from shower fog. You hung

my Picasso with gold
garland, balanced an egg
basket on Wyatt Earp's tomb
stone, rumbled your bullhorn
like a tractor with bad
fuel, and then came to my door
with your toupee crooked
and everyone laughing.

When I think of you I whisper
to the candle flame so it flickers.
      It was you

                what's so terrible is I thought
                his bubbling brain looked
                like a hundred piñatas
                on the sidewalk   they burst
                to reveal more piñatas
                      then those piñatas burst
                and those burst too   piñatas
                piñatas piñatas   riga needs
                more piñatas—said the police
                man—where will we find
                      more piñatas

      who gave me directions
to the Hofbräuhaus man
in Lederhosen. I owe you a beer
stein and another dance. Crack—

come with me while we crack
an egg from the basket at the
graveyard, snap off a statue's penis
at the Pushkin, use it as a swizzle
stick to mix the egg
well with our brew.

Withdrawal

Without my daily dose
of Dolly I write poems
about squids in minis,
mirrors in Maria,
carafe shards in my hair,

and Lawrence Welk chisels
Kathy Ireland out of a half-eaten
Klondike Bar, her sickly skinny fudge
legs melt down a playground slide
in the hot Columbia sun and
drip like Beethoven's piano notes.

Wayne Newton pours liquid
detergent in the courthouse fountain,
dances and splashes in the growing
bubbles with the Wicked Witch
of the West, leaves a soapy
loop around her lips
when he kisses her,

and Elvis howls
Ain't nothin' but a Jolene
while my accordion flamencos
with Dr. Frank N. Furter at the picture
show, straight through the fuzzy credits
like wet shoes bouncing
down a laundry chute.

A Fitting Finale

I don't want to die a normal
    death ninety-four years old peaceful
        in my sleep. I grew thick skin
    when I was two, so how about a great
white gobbles me up skinny

    dipping the Florida Gulf with Dolly?
        Newspaper headlines whittle a soap-sliver
            moon for my funeral after I bungee Golden
    Gate Bridge with a twist tie rope
from Alcatraz cafeteria.

        No one will say I died
           a boring death.   Is the Milky Way
                wrapping arms in heaven around mountain
            laurel fairies ?   How about I fall
    into a bus engine and wind

through firing-chamber
    pistons until oily chains
        of stephen sausages—twisted!—
    flop out the exhaust pipe? What
a proud woman I'll make

my mother. Cut my hair
    with diamond scissors, glue orange
        blue feathers to the undertaker's bald
    head, turn my hearing aid up
so it squeals when my rosewood

                        casket closes.

Acknowledgments

Credit is due to the editors of the following, in which some of the poems from this collection first appeared:

32 Poems: "Foxie's"
Barely South Review: "Weight"
Best of the Net 2006 (Sundress): "Sunday After"
Boxcar Poetry Review: "Sunday After"
Boxcar Poetry Review 2006 Anthology: "Sunday After"
Blue Earth Review: "Did I Tell You About the Homeless Man I Saw in Riga?"
Clemson Poetry Review: "The Reward of the Gift Waits Until Morning"
The Comstock Review: "Tybee Still Life"
A Cup of Poems and a Side of Prose: "Withdrawal"
Dislocate: "In the Village the Night Before We Flew to Europe"
The Fourth River: "Where It's Shallow by the Island on Rest Lake"
Interrobang?!: "Elitist in Central Georgia"
Natural Bridge: "Coronado"
Paper Street: "Learning the Motions"
Pinyon: "Hooked"
Red Earth Review: "Losing the Girl I Took to Dollywood Isn't Hard to Master"
Rock Salt Plum Review: "Tonight Near Sunset Crater"
Rougarou: "I'm the New Lover Helping Her Try On the Unused Oleg Cassini"
The Southern Poetry Anthology Volume V: Georgia (Texas Review P): "The Great Chicago Earthquake of 2002"
Taj Mahal Review: "Sunday After"
Talking River: "Night Visitors"
Tapestry: "Dolly Floats"
Wisconsin Poets' Calendar: "Talking in My Sleep in the Northwoods"

For their involvement and help in the writing of both this collection and *The Follower's Tale*, I especially want to thank Susan Firer, Maurice Kilwein Guevara, William Harrold, Jim Hazard, James Liddy, Sheila Roberts, and Marilyn Taylor. You've all taught me well. For sharing with me art, smokes, drinks, and pizza through all stages of the writing process, I owe gratitude to Mike Driscoll, David Duhr, Zeke Jarvis, and Joanne Staudacher. Thank you, Harrell Gabehart and Patric Parkey, for inviting me to Texas to have supper with Dolly's clothes. Thank you, Sherman Alexie, for "Ode to Jolene" and for the encouragement to write a second collection inspired by Dolly. Several of the poems here and in *The Follower's Tale* were born over good food, wine, and cigars in different parts of the world with Marc Emmelmann. Thank you for your generous Hilton HHonors account—I've lost count of all the places we've used it. And thanks to you, Carl Jenkinson, for the title of this book and everything else that started with "Drive My Urn to Dollywood," including the moonshine. I am particularly beholden to Natasha Chisdes, Mickey Mogensen, James Morton, and Paula Sergi for their friendship and eagle-eyed reading of early versions of these poems. Thanks are also due to Gordon State College for funding and to Ed Whitelock for assistance and support in writing and promoting my work. Without my family I am nothing. I hope you all know how grateful I am for you. Speaking of my family, thank you, Margie Littell, for Boog's B & B. Finally, special gratitude and love to Siobhán Hutson and Jessie Lendennie of Salmon Poetry, and to Dolly Parton.

STEPHEN ROGER POWERS started writing poetry thirteen years ago to pass time in the middle of the night when he was too energized to sleep after coming off the stage in comedy clubs around the American Midwest. He is the author of *The Follower's Tale*, also published by Salmon. He hasn't done stand-up in a long time, but every once in a while he finds avenues for the performer he was born to be. He was an extra in *Joyful Noise* with Queen Latifah and Dolly Parton, and he can be seen if you know just where to look.